Snapchat

———— ✧❧❧✧ ————

*Snapchat Marketing Strategies and
Secrets to Maximize Your Brand Reach*

By Logan King

Table of Contents

Introduction

I would like to thank you for purchasing this book.

One of the most popular social media platforms in the world is Snapchat and rightly so. It helps people in connecting with their friends and family and it does so with the help of the latest pictures and videos.

Snapchat was launched in the year 2011 and it was meant to serve as a platform for picture social media. This app helps in encouraging people to post and share their pictures and videos with their friends and family members. After the lapse of a few seconds, these pictures will self-destruct and this is the unique feature of Snapchat.

Snapchat is extremely popular amongst teens as well as young adults. It isn't however restricted to just this and can be made use of increasing your business potential. It is indeed a perfect promotional tool for selling products and services.

Many companies, regardless of their size, are not making use of this platform for selling their products. If you happen to be a businessman looking for a manner in which you can make use of this app's popularity, then you have selected the right book. It will guide you through all the details of this app and help you in understanding its uses for people as well as businesses.

We will take a look at the process of getting started with Snapchat and show you the ways in which a business can make the most of it.

If you aren't on Snapchat yet, then you are definitely missing out on a lot of fun. Once you have finished reading this book, you will be eager to put this app to good use. So, hop on board and let us explore this app. Let us get started!

Chapter One:

Getting Started With Snapchat

In this chapter, let us take a look at all the basics of Snapchat and how you can get started with this app.

What is Snapchat?

In the year 2011, Snapchat was launched. This was a social media application or an app. The main purpose of this app was to help people to share photos as well as videos that would automatically self-destruct within seconds of the receiver receiving it and opening it.

This is the feature that sets Snapchat apart when compared to other social media apps. It helps in maintaining privacy. Ever since it was launched, Snapchat has become extremely popular and today, it is considered to be one of the most widely used social media applications. Snapchat is available for all mobile platforms and this app was created so that people could express themselves in a better manner.

Celebrities, socialites, famous personalities, practically everyone has joined Snapchat and this just adds to its appeal. Snapchat is not only easy to download, but it is also easy to use.

When was it launched?

Snapchat was launched in the year 2011, and it has been updated multiple times since then. The present version is popular and has been designed to suit the preferences of a great number of users.

As per the statistics available, there are more than 700 million snaps that are shared on a daily basis on Snapchat. This means that there are more than 900 snaps being shared on average per second. These statistics show the popularity of Snapchat. Snapchat is regarded as one of the best apps for sending and receiving pictures.

Facebook had made an offer to Snapchat for amalgamation; however, this offer was declined by its creators since they didn't want to jump on board the commercial vehicle. Facebook then tried to launch an app along the lines of Snapchat, known as Slingshot. However, Slingshot failed to match up to the popularity of Snapchat.

What is its purpose?

In today's world, where everyone wants to share pictures and videos, an app that is solely dedicated to this purpose is, in fact, a perfect choice. However, privacy issues have become a major worry for people these days especially when they are sharing their pictures with others.

This is one problem that Snapchat has successfully capitalized on. It was created with an intention of helping people send or share their pictures with others anywhere across the globe, without having to worry about the privacy risks. The pictures will self-destruct within a few seconds and this doesn't give the receiver a chance to store them.

This feature is the biggest selling point of this app!

Who can use Snapchat?

Originally, the audiences that Snapchat catered for were teens and young adults. This app has features like the addition of filters that can be made use of for modifying or enhancing the picture quality.

This feature became instantly popular with college students and office goers. However, with the passage of time, even businesses began to see the potential of Snapchat for promoting their products and services. They began making use of it for promoting their goods to consumers. They also started to make use of this app for increasing the popularity of their brand.

Many businesses now make use of Snapchat for expanding their customer base and also for increasing their sales. You can start gaining the same benefits by reading the different tips and tricks that have been mentioned in this book.

How does Snapchat work?

At present, Snapchat is considered to be amongst one of the best apps that are available for keeping in touch with friends and family. This is a simple application that allows its users to share pictures and videos with great ease. Snapchat also provides a platform for people to chat with, or message, each other.

This makes it incredibly easy for people to keep in touch with each other and also for sharing pictures and videos with each other. The friends and followers of a user will be able to look at the pictures and videos that the user has shared and they can share their own with their followers as well.

Getting started with Snapchat

It is really easy to get started with Snapchat. Here are the steps for getting started with it.

Step 1: The first step is to download this app from the app store. This application is available on Android, iOS, and windows app stores. Once the app has been downloaded, you will need to open it on your phone.

Step 2: Once you have opened it, the app will ask you to fill in certain details like your email address, a password, and your birthday. These details are compulsory and you will need to enter them. The minimum age limit for using this application is 13 years. If you aren't 13, then you will be redirected to an alternative app known as Snapkidz.

Step 3: The app will then proceed to verify your identity by asking you a few questions. These are quite simple and are mostly visual questions.

Step 4: The next step would be to add your contacts to your list. Snapchat will ask you to grant access to your contact list. By doing so, you are automatically transferring all your contacts to your Snapchat. However, if you aren't keen on doing so, then you can modify the friend list and proceed to add only those people who you would want to have on your list.

Step 5: The next step would be to pick your personal preferences. There is an option available for managing the filters, camera flash, reply tab, texts and so on. You also have the option of selecting those with whom you would want to send and receive snaps.

Step 6: The next step would be to make use of your phone's camera for taking snaps. These snaps can be shared with other people. The app has got automatic access to the camera and it allows you to take pictures. You have the option of adding a tagline or a short caption for personalizing the photo. There are different filters that you can choose from and these filters will help in enhancing the appeal of the pictures taken.

Step 7: The next step would be to send the snap to a person with whom you would wish to share it. Select the people with whom you would want to share the snap from your friend list and send it.

Step 8: You will be able to receive snaps as well. You will simply need to go to received snaps for finding the pictures that you were sent.

Step 9: Snapchat has also got the option of adding a story. A story could be a video or even a picture that would let your followers know what you have been doing. A story lasts for 24 hours and it self-destructs like the snaps after the expiration of the agreed time period.

Step 10: You have the option of even starting a chat session with a friend. This feature is similar to that of any other chat messengers available. The messages will appear one above the other. However, unlike the other messengers, you won't be allowed to read the previous chats once you close the window.

Myths Surrounding Snapchat

Snapchat is for people, not businesses

This is a very common misconception that surrounds Snapchat. People believe that Snapchat is exclusively designed for people and will not hold good for businesses. However, this is only a myth as it is great for businesses to promote their products and services. Companies will find it convenient to come up with strategies using pictures and videos to reach out to an audience.

Through the course of this book, we will look at the many ways in which you can use Snapchat for business purposes.

Snapchat is overshadowed by other platforms

This is another misconception doing the rounds. People believe that Snapchat is not as popular as Facebook or Twitter. However, this is a wrong comparison as they are not all the same. Facebook and Twitter are different from Snapchat in that they are used to promote messages.

Snapchat, on the other hand, is exclusively for picture promotions. This works better as people will be drawn to pictures as compared to just text. Snapchat is in a league of its own and not affected by competition from other sites.

Snapchat does not allow marketing

Snapchat has a feature known as storytelling where people can add in a series of pictures to tell a story. This feature is great as companies can post a series of pictures about a campaign or even their products. This allows them to market their products effectively.

It is a great tool to use to send across a message to the audience, as they will be able to relate to it better. In fact, many companies, big and small, now use Snapchat stories as a means to campaign their products.

It will take time to establish oneself

This will depend on the type of campaigns that are being used. If the campaigns are interesting and you manage to score a lot of followers then you will establish yourself pretty quickly. You must ensure that you keep your content up to date and provide your audiences with interesting material. Only then will you be able to capitalize on Snapchat's success as a promotional tool.

Snapchat is still relatively new to the world of business promotion and does not promote it as aggressively as Facebook and Twitter so it will take a little time for you to use Snapchat to promote business.

I am on Instagram so I don't need Snapchat

Instagram and Snapchat are not the same. In fact, they are extremely diverse and do not clash on any level. Snapchat provides you with a platform where pictures are automatically destroyed after a certain point of time. This makes it ideal for many types of businesses and allows them to come up with new campaigns every now and then.

The features provided on Snapchat are also quite different from the ones on Instagram. Therefore, if you want a great platform to promote your business then Snapchat is the one for you.

Chapter Two:

Snapchat- Future of Social Media

Social media platforms like Facebook, Twitter, and LinkedIn still have a strong hold on the world of social media due to the sheer number of users. There are a handful of other social media apps and platforms that are trying to create a place for themselves. Snapchat happens to be amongst these and it has the strongest potential too.

It not only has the capacity for building a user base that could rival the major channels mentioned above, but it is also creating sufficient influence the manner in which other platforms are developing. Let us take a look at the reasons why Snapchat has such a good potential.

Younger demographic

Statistics recorded by Snapchat show that above 71% of their users are under the age of 35. There are three main reasons why it is believed that the younger generations are responsible for driving the latest trends. The first reason is that they hold a major chunk of the buying power and this tends to attract most of the companies and organizations who use it.

The second reason is that they are the most adaptable of the lot and can easily adapt to new platforms. The third and the major reason is that there is a likelihood that they will favor the platforms they aged with and will bring the same into the mainstream.

Privacy

One of the main reasons for the growth and success of Snapchat is the manner in which it treats user content. The snaps are automatically deleted permanently after a set period of time. This helps in ensuring user privacy. There have been major security and data breaches in major companies; users are skeptical about what they are willing to share. Platforms that can identify such threats and address these will grow over the next few years.

Innovation

Snapchat keeps on adding new features and functions. There is no sign that it will slow down anytime soon. The new features that Snapchat keeps on adding aren't drawn from those of its competitors. These features haven't been mimicked or mainstream.

Dominance

Mobile devices are becoming extremely popular and their popularity is increasing by the day. Most of the popular platforms have a desktop and mobile application like Facebook and Twitter. Snapchat has developed an app that is specifically designed for mobile phones. They have added different features to improve functionality like vertical videos.

Snapchat is trying to make the most of the medium for which it was developed.

Learning curve

The learning curve that is necessary for making use of the app is one of its most counterintuitive features. It is easy to start using Snapchat; however, it will take a while before you have sufficient experience for making the best use of this platform. It not only encourages new users but it also rewards long-term use. This enables it to create a perfect learning curve that helps in retaining users.

Immediate posts

Immediate post or in the moment posts are quite popular now. Snapchat and Instagram cater to this craze. Even social media giants like Facebook are getting this on board via functions like Facebook Live.

Chapter Three:

Connecting With Your Snapchat Followers

Most of the brands and companies tend to allocate time and energy for creating content that will help them in engaging their customers. In this chapter, let us take a look at the different ways in which companies and brands can connect with their followers on Snapchat.

Finding your creative edge

Snapchat is really helpful for companies that have got a message to share. It is not just for companies that are trying to increase the customer traffic to their website or for increasing downloads.

If you think that there's a story behind your brand, then Snapchat will definitely come in handy. You will be able to create a foothold for yourself by showcasing your brand in a different light. It could be through creative storytelling, celebrity meet-ups, concerts or even adventures.

Make sure that you are telling the story of your brand by posting content from such an environment or surroundings that would represent it.

Do not over advertise

It is incredibly easy to simply swipe down or even tap through the stories on Snapchat. Therefore, the story that you are posting should be such that it can easily grab the viewer's attention and it should be fast paced. The audience shouldn't lose interest. If you want to make good use of Snapchat, then keep making use of the added filters and emojis.

Get as creative as possible. Make the store seem "cool" and make viewers eager for more. You will need to keep posting unique content on a daily basis and you will need to engage as well as build your audience by including interesting content that will get your message across.

Spokesperson

It is incredibly important that you find the "right" spokesperson for representing your brand. It is important that you can tie up with someone who has got an audience and also knows how to make the most of this app.

There are a lot of social media influencers ranging from musicians and singers to actors. Just having a large audience base is not important, they will also need to know the best manner in which they can optimize the app and make the most of it. They will need to be able to engage the audience too. You wouldn't want to tie up with a person who is simply trying to report their statistics to their boss.

You will need someone who knows his or her way around this app. It could be an individual or an agency and knowing the content and the manner in which it is posted are vital.

Increasing user engagement

Audience engagement can be increased by posting stories or a collection of videos or photos on Snapchat that can be replayed for a period of 24 hours. However, with the introduction of the new feature that helps in replying to a specific snap or a video by swiping the bottom of the display and by opening a new chat the app is more interactive.

This means that the marketers will now be able to receive feedback for the snaps that they are posting. This is a brilliant manner in which you will be able to see if your campaign is working or not. You can snap back your audience, open their snaps, include them in your story, and give them freebies too. This will keep them engaged and they will be excited by what they are doing too.

Chapter Four:

What the Snapchat Terms Mean

Snapchat definitely has got its own jargon. When you're aware of this, you will be able to communicate more naturally.

Snaps

This refers to the individual pictures that are sent and received in Snapchat. Snaps are shared with your friends and family members. The same snap can be sent across to multiple Snapchatters. All those who make use of Snapchat are referred to as the Snapchatters. These snaps don't last for more than ten seconds before they self-destruct. You will also have the option of selecting the time for which a snap would be available for viewing.

Snapback

This is the term that is used when a reply is given to a particular snap. To put it simply, it is the response that you would have received from the other Snapchatters for the snap that you sent them. You can also measure the number of snapbacks that you have given and those who have received it as well.

Story

A story would be a collection of pictures or even snaps that can be added one by one to the account. These can then be viewed by your followers as many times as they would like to. However, a story will be available for only 24 hours. Each story could be a narrative of a specific event that you were a part of or any activity in which you participated. You can also view the stories posted by your friends in the story section present in your account.

Scores

There are statistics that are provided to a particular individual based on the number of snaps received, sent, snapbacks and so on. All these different things are taken into account for providing the score of an individual. You also have the option of viewing your friend's score as well to know the number of snaps that haven't been sent or received.

Snapcode

Snapcodes are a really easy way for adding new friends to your account. You can make use of your phone for scanning and adding new friends or users to your account. It is not only simple, but it is quick as well. You can access your Snapcode by tapping on the ghost icon that you notice on your phone.

Snapstreak

This refers to the consecutive number of days for which you have been sharing your snaps with your friend on Snapchat. It is incredibly important that you keep sharing as many photos as possible. This is the main feature of this app.

Friends and Followers

There is a huge difference between friends and followers on your Snapchat account. The individuals who have been added from your contact list are referred to as friends. You get the option of adding friends to your friend list by clicking on the plus symbol that appears on the right hand corner of the page.

Followers are the people who have started following you, but you aren't following them. These names will show up on your account as a list of followers.

Lenses

This refers to the different modifications that you can make use of for the pictures taken. These are real-time effects that can be easily added onto your snaps. There are different filters that you can choose from and each of these is unique. These lenses are free and they can be made use of for modifying your pictures. These things change frequently and you will not get bored with these.

Filters

Filters are the overlays that can be added onto your pictures. These are meant to make your pictures seem more interesting. There are different filters that you can choose from and each of these provides a different effect. The filters are extremely popular since they allow you to place fun pictures about the location on your photos.

Chapter Four: What the Snapchat Terms Mean

There are certain popular acronyms that you should know for convenience sake. FTFY means fixed that for you. If you have fixed something for someone and want to apologize for the same then you can make use of FTFY. This can also be made use of for modifying a picture. HIFW stands for how I felt when.

This signifies a feeling that you have experienced. This is usually used for signifying a funny situation. JSYK stands for just so you know; it is also used as an alternative for FYI. TIL stands for today, I learned and SMH stands for shaking my head. These are some of the acronyms that are commonly used.

Chapter Five:

Building Your Brand Using Snapchat

Wondering how you can make use of Snapchat for your business? Do you want to create a deeper bond with your Snapchat followers? In this chapter, you will learn about the different ways in which you can make use of Snapchat for your business.

Staging an influencer reveal

McDonald's is a global fast food giant and they aren't just for the redheaded clown and their meals with toys. Before launching their new bacon clubhouse sandwich, a couple of professional athletes like LeBron James gave all the users a 'behind the scenes' look. They partnered with athletes for promoting their product. McDonald's did not share the results of this promotional activity.

It is safe to assume that it went well given that it went on for quite a while. Their promotion was pushed to other social media like Twitter, where the users were asked to follow back. McDonald's has over 3 million followers on their Twitter handle. The same philosophy that McDonald's made use of can be applied to any company. Give your customers a sneak peek of how things get done.

Even if your marketing budget happens to be a small fraction of the McDonald's one, the buyers will still be interested in getting to know what is happening.

Supporting an account takeover

If you want your message to be seen, then you can allow an influential Snapchatter to take over your user account. You might not have connections with millions of followers. However, even being able to rope in a local authority can be of great help.

For instance, a clothing retailer Wet Seal launched a Snapchat campaign and the same was taken over by MsMeghanMakeup, a Snapchatter who has over 300,000 followers. Her influence helped the campaign.

Sharing your promo codes

You can provide your Snapchat followers with Snapchat exclusive coupons or promo codes for improving your brand visibility. For instance, the frozen yogurt chain- 16 made use of their Snapchat followers and the instant photo feature for promoting their brand. They were also amongst the first brand that made use of the coupon offers on Snapchat. The yogurt company acquired new customers by promoting certain specific locations of their stores at a particular time.

People would need to get there and snap photos of themselves or their friends eating the frozen yogurt from 16 Handles. They would immediately receive a coupon code for a discount from

16% to 100%. However, there's a catch. This would be valid for ten seconds.

Giving VIP access

It took several weeks before the photos from New York Fashion week would trickle down to the consumers. However, with Snapchat, followers can be provided with instant updates. Snapchat can be made use of for sharing instant updates from any major events.

The editor in chief of Lucky Magazine had shared the snaps of different models while strutting on the runway. This revolutionized the manner in which people received the latest information and images from iconic events in real time. Your followers will be able to see the proceedings from any event if you give them a VIP access to it on Snapchat.

Featuring your followers

Make sure that your Snapchat feed isn't always about yourself. Include your followers in it and you can also involve them in the process of content creation. The online food ordering service GrubHub launched their first marketing campaign on Snapchat in 2013.

They used to feature their weekly content and would include content gathered from users, any giveaways, and promotions as well. This projected a 20% increase in their number of followers.

Providing a demo

The online retailing giant Amazon made use of Snapchat for not only giving a demo about their voice-activated speaker Echo, but also made use of it promotional purposes as well. This helped in providing some clarity to the confused consumers when Echo was launched.

It managed to gather more than 6100 mentions in less than 4 hours. If your brand has recently launched a new technology or a product, then you can make use of Snapchat for providing a virtual guide to the manner in which the product is to be used.

Partnering with influencers

You can add some popular Snapchatters and then get them to follow you too. This will definitely help in increasing your follower base and their followers will take to you as well. Search for some of the popular ones in your area and start following them. You can also email them and then add your Snapchat code in the email or your name so that it will be easy for them to follow you.

Addressing any relevant issue

Don't be afraid to be real while using this media. For instance, the campaign run by Dove is an example of this. The soap brand Dove appealed to the older section of the society till it reached out to the younger lot by making use of Snapchat. Over two hours, 30 women got to chat with psychologists and other ambassadors of this brand on Snapchat and they got to share their ideas and thoughts about the issues on self-esteem. These suggestions were taken into consideration by Dove.

Post daily

It is incredibly important that you keep posting on a daily basis and that you keep your audiences regularly updated. This is the only way in which you can keep them coming back for more and pique their interest.

Think of different things that you can do to grab their attention. You can keep track of what other companies do and try to match up. It won't be easy. However, once you have managed to get the hang of it, then you will definitely see a positive change in your business.

Public stories

Make sure that all the stories that you are posting are public. This is incredibly important since people will need to go through what you are sharing with them.

The stories will automatically destruct themselves after 24 hours and then you will need to add a new one. However, if you want to maintain exclusivity by sharing certain things that only a few customers can view, then you have that option available too. This will definitely help in making them feel special and improve your brand name.

Other platforms

It is a good idea to link all of your social media accounts. This would include your profiles on Twitter, Facebook, and LinkedIn too. It becomes easier to share information and make the content more relatable for your followers. Continuing the same campaign across different platforms will ensure that there is some uniformity and it will help in connecting better with the audience.

Expand contacts

Snapchat accesses your contact list and helps in adding friends. It will help you in expanding your contact list and thereby increase your reach. Make use of these leads and send messages to your friends. They will be able to see any updates posted by you and know the content that they are being offered.

You shouldn't let go of a single opportunity that will help you in reigning in a potential customer. Tap into the friend lists of your friends and acquaintances for increasing your following.

Groups

You should make sure that you are a part of appropriate groups on various other social media networks. This will help you in staying in contact with others who can be useful for your business. There are various forums available online where you can leave your Snapchat name for others to add you. You can start bringing up any topic that you want and start a discussion on these groups.

Variety

The pictures and stories you post shouldn't be predictable. Post things that will surprise and excite your audience. You will need to add value to the content that you are posting. If they find similar content elsewhere, it would defeat the purpose. Keep things interesting and unique for your audience.

Up to date

Make sure that the content and the material that you are making use of for your snaps is up-to-date. They should feature the latest filters and lenses. Making use of the old and redundant features will simply make it boring for your audience. Posting viral content will help with numbers too.

Chapter Six:

Metrics to Monitor When Using Snapchat

Snapchat is a great platform that should be explored by marketers and it is so for a good reason. There are more than 6 billion daily video views that have been delivered by Snapchat on a daily basis. That's a massive number. Facebook has about 8 million daily video views and YouTube around 4 billion.

What is different about Snapchat is that all these views are from mobile devices exclusively. This is a big opportunity for marketers and a platform available for brands to tell their stories. About three-quarters of the users in the US are over 18 years and more and more users belonging to the 20's are joining Snapchat too.

There are many marketers who have been spending time to just get used to this platform, but there is one thing that is still confusing people. This is the manner in which success of particular content can be measured on Snapchat.

Marketers keep struggling to make sense of the data that is available to them. It is completely understandable why they wouldn't know how to analyze data on a new platform like Snapchat without any formal analytics.

Marketers shouldn't focus much on the followers they have and should instead focus on the number of people who are lapping up the stories posted. Let us take a look at the major metrics that you will need to monitor while making use of Snapchat.

Total Unique Views

The total unique views stands for the number of people who have opened the first frame in the Snapchat story you posted for the duration of at least one second. This can be done by taking a look at the number of people who have opened the first snap of your story in the 24-hour time frame.

Users are allowed to post as many snaps as they want and each snap can't be more than 10 seconds long. Users get to watch a snap story for the duration of the 24 hours for which it is available. One really interesting thing about the Total Unique Views metrics is on par with what Snapchat provides.

If you have paid Snapchat for running ads on your platform, then you have paid for running a 10-second video in the story. You can create as many ten-second videos as you want to. This means that the individual ads that you can create will help in delivering more content and engaging your audience more than a 10-second ad.

Total Story Completions

A story on Snapchat can be just one snap or even 100 snaps. The best storytellers make use of the 24-hour time frame available on Snapchat for stringing together multiple snaps for creating a single video. When you have posted one single story that has multiple frames, then you will need to look at the number of people who have viewed the last snap. This will help in measuring the number of people who have actually watched the whole video and have consumed the story.

Completion Rate

A Snapchat is quite similar to a storybook. It has an introduction, then there's a story, and an end to that story as well. Thankfully, Snapchat allows its users to see the number of people who have viewed every chapter. The completion rate is the portion of people who have started viewing the story as compared to the number of people who viewed the ending of the story.

Facebook and YouTube tend to think of completion rate as a way to measure engagement. The audience on Snapchat tends to view the entire content at one go even though the brands keep on posting all day long.

Screenshots

On Snapchat, unlike other social media platforms, there is no option for liking, commenting, or sharing anything. However, users have the option of checking the number the people who have taken the screenshots of their snaps. This can be made use of as a tool for engagement as well.

For instance, you can also encourage people to screenshot their choices in a "select your own adventure" type of a story. Alternatively, you can also make use of screenshots as a method of polling. You can ask people to screenshot their personal favorite among the product designs available for collecting their feedback. You can record the number of screenshots of particular things and then follow up with your users.

Chapter Seven:

Advantages of Using Snapchat

T he best photo-sharing app that is currently available is Snapchat. In this chapter, let us take a look at the different advantages that are available for making use of Snapchat.

Point of view

The biggest advantage of making use of Snapchat is that it helps in acquiring a firsthand perspective of a person's world. Friends and family will be able to see things in the same manner in which you are seeing them.

This will help in sharing of more information. Your audience will be able to see things how you see them. They will be able to see it at the same time that you are seeing it and this makes it more special.

Timing

The stories posted on Snapchat only last for 24 hours and this make it incredibly easy and convenient for people. It is suited for those who do not like maintaining too many pictures or videos. Their snaps will disappear once the designated time is up.

This is a great way in which you can maintain your privacy and yet keep in touch with your audience. The pictures won't be available long enough for someone to misuse it. Even if someone takes a screenshot of something you sent and you will get a notification if this happens.

Buzz

This is a great platform for creating buzz about something. The app will allow you to create short videos that can be used as a teaser for something. You can create a short preview for creating a buzz about an event amongst your followers.

This works really well for all those who want to promote themselves or their businesses. You can make viral videos and easily build an audience.

Ease

It is really easy to make use of Snapchat. As you would have gathered by now, this is one of the most user-friendly apps that are available in the market at present. It can be used for chatting and sharing pictures. The app is user-friendly and the user interface is fun to use.

Snapchat for business

Snapchat is a really good way in which you can enrich your business and enhance any business opportunities that are available for you. This is a great platform if you want to cover any live event. The audience can be involved in the form of contests and live events.

This will help in keeping your audience interested and also increase your audience base. There are many companies that are using this platform for creating a buzz about their products and services. A small trailer or preview of what is in store for customers can be given and this will definitely help in capturing their attention and intriguing your audience.

The average age group of users includes teens and goes up to 34 years. This means that it would be really easy to target the younger audience and connect with them. This is also perhaps the most difficult age group to please. Snapchat makes it easier for brands to reach out and connect with this audience.

You can post behind the scene photos and videos to make your audience feel more connected to the brand. This is also an ideal platform for conducting any giveaway. A giveaway will help your consumers feel more interested and this would be the reward for their loyalty. Snapchat is a great way to connect with them. You will learn more about making use of Snapchat for marketing your business or brand in the next chapter.

Chapter Eight:

Using Snapchat for Business

Snapchat is an incredibly useful tool for all businesses and it helps in the retention of customers as well. It was indeed launched with the intent of targeting teens and young adults. However, it soon became an extremely popular means of promoting products and services too. We took a look at some of the ways in which Snapchat is helpful for a business. Let us take a few more advantages and the steps for setting up a Snapchat account for a business.

Snapchat is considered to be amongst the most used social networking media around the world. There are more than 100 million active users registered on it and this makes it a really good platform for promoting businesses and brands on it. However, many companies still tend to prefer Facebook and Twitter for promoting themselves.

A study shows that only about 2% of the top companies make use of Snapchat for advertising themselves. This shows that there is a great scope for advertising on here for a business to exploit. Upcoming businesses can capitalize on this opportunity since they would no longer be a part of the rat race with all the other big business houses. This is also a good opportunity for all those businesses that are well established and are looking for a new manner in which they can increase their audience base.

Snapchat is providing them with a way in which they can increase their sales. A well-defined timeline is another major advantage of making use of Snapchat. This means that the audience will not get confused or distracted by any clutter and all the snaps will have their necessary space.

It is important to take into consideration that making use of Snapchat for the purposes of business will be different from making use of it as a social networking tool for interacting with your friends and family. You will need to adopt a different approach in this case. This consideration should be given attention since people should know that they are interacting with a business or a brand and not just an individual.

That being said, it shouldn't be too serious or the audience will get bored. It is important to represent the business in the best possible way and provide a chance for the audience to connect with it. Here are the steps that you will need to follow for setting up a Snapchat profile for your business.

Step 1: The first step would be to installation of the app. Follow the same instructions that have been mentioned in Chapter 1.

Step 2: While you are setting up your account, make sure that it is as professional as it can be. The name of your business or company should be the Snapchat name. This will enable people to know that it is the official profile of the company. The profile picture could be the logo of your company. For instance, Disney makes use of their official logo to be placed as their profile picture in the center of the ghost. If your logo is not recognizable, then you can add the name of your company to that.

Step 3: Now you will need to add your friends. This will help in creating an instant base of audience and will make sure that you are starting off on the right foot. They will be able to see what you are posting and then provide you with their feedback. Based on all this, you can make the necessary changes to your campaign for making your content more interesting.

Step 4: You will need to find other companies and then start following them. This will help you in gathering information about what they are into and the marketing strategies that they are making use of. You will need to keep a track of the strategies made use of by your business and also the things they are posting. This will definitely go a long way in helping you come up with better promotional campaigns for your business.

Step 5: You will need to select and build your own audience base. This is an incredibly important step of this process. You will need to acquire as many followers as possible if you want to be able to reach out to a large audience. This is akin to finding as many Twitter followers as possible on Twitter.

Step 6: You can start following some famous celebrities on Snapchat. Doing this will help you in improving your audience base. If you have any personal contacts with such celebrities, then you can request them to add you to their friend list for improving your visibility.

Step 7: You will need to start creating snaps and stories that will appeal to your audience. This will help you a great deal. After reaching a certain point, then you can start concentrating on building a stronger connection with a smaller target audience and build specific strategies to solely cater for them.

Step 8: Make sure that you have set a fixed time for updating your snaps and stories. This will enable people to know when they can expect an update and they will also get used to checking the snaps from your business at a particular time.

Chapter Nine:

Snapchat Marketing Strategies

S napchat is a great stage for you to market the products and services offered by your brand or business. Here, we look at some Snapchat strategies for enhancing your business.

Contests

Organizing exclusive contests on your Snapchat is indeed a great idea. People will be able to take part in them and relate better to your business. The contests can be anything from choosing a caption for your pictures or putting up pictures with the product sold by your business.

All of these are great ways to promote your Snapchat account and market products and services. The giveaway after the contest ends should be unique or worthy so that people put their best effort. Announce the contest on all your different social media platforms in advance so that people know when to take part in it.

Events

Announcing events for your customers through Snapchat will be of help. The platform provides a great opportunity to bring your customers together. Post invites for them and ask them to screenshot it. Whoever has it can appear at the event. This makes for a great way to engage your audience and get them to RSVP to the event.

Again, announce it on all your social media platforms so that people known about it in advance. Ask them at the event whether they liked the concept and would like to have more of it. Plan your future campaigns based on their response.

Tie-ups

It is a good idea to tie up with other companies on Snapchat. Doing so will help you exchange followers. For example, post a picture and ask your followers to screenshot it. The same can work as a coupon to get discount for your partner's products and vice versa.

However, remember to tie up with companies that have equal or more *followers* than you as that will be fair game. Once you have a thriving run you will be able to tie up with others a lot easier. You need not limit it to just one partner and tie up with as many as you like.

Offers

Provide exclusive discounts and other offers on your Snapchat only. This can be something like coupon codes to gain a discount, buy one get one free etc. These offers should be exclusively available on your Snapchat account alone and not anywhere else. However, you can advertise about it on your other platforms in order to tell your customers about the same.

Try to vary the offers every now and then in order to keep the audience engaged. Look at what some of the offers by rival companies and match up to it. Again, come up with innovative ways to announce the offers on your Snapchat account.

Previews

Snapchat is a great place for you to offer a sneak-peak into your upcoming products and services. Add a picture or video of what is to come and your audience will be on the edge of their seats. Incorporate a game here also and make it interesting.

Ask them to take a screenshot of a particular product from the newest collection that they can win. Similarly, think up other ways in which to market your products using Snapchat to reach out to a bigger audience.

Media Exclusives

A nice trick to increase followers is to offer exclusive products through Snapchat alone. For example, only your followers on Snapchat will have access to a particular collection. These can be different in terms of color, design, or pattern. You will have to tell them clearly that they will be exclusively available through Snapchat alone and not anywhere else. Consider introducing a whole different line of products that are only available through your Snapchat account.

Merchandize

Offer customers exclusive merchandise. This merchandise will carry your company's name and logo. You also have the choice to add their name or any other information that they would like to have on the merchandise. Customizing products for customers helps them keep coming back for more and Snapchat can play a part in it.

Celebrities

Celebrities work like magic in terms of garnering attention. Start following celebrities and get them to follow you. This will create a buzz about your company. Keep your best friend list open for people see, as they will know who is on your list. The same extends to having popular Snapchatters on your list.

Others will be able to see who you have and enhance your account's appeal. There are many fashion models to follow. It would be great if you could get one of them to wear or use your products and use the same on your account.

Rewards

Offer your customers rewards such as incentives for following your Snapchat account. That will ensure you increase the number of followers. The rewards can be discount coupons or store credit that the followers can use to get discounts and other offers. Announce the same in advance and on other platforms as well.

Referrals

Offer rewards for referrals as well. This is a trick that many businesses now use to attract followers. Announce a reward for those that bring in other followers. The reward should be lucrative enough to attract people and keep them interested.

Chapter Ten:

Leveraging Social Media for Making Money

Up until now, we have been looking at the different ways in which social media can be made use of by a business. In this chapter, let us take a look at the ways in which an individual can make use of social media for making more money.

Writing sponsored posts

There are many websites, businesses and brands that would offer their followers and their customer's opportunities for sharing sponsored posts for promoting the products and services offered by them. This is a great way in which you can earn money by making use of social media. You needn't have any products of your own for sale.

The first step for getting started with sponsored posts would be to grow your follower base on multiple social media platforms such as Facebook, Twitter, Instagram, or even Snapchat. You will need to have a good flow of traffic to your blog if you want companies to offer you money for writing about them. You will need to have more than 5000 page views every month for your blog.

Once you have managed to acquire a good number of followers and readers, then you can start making money through sponsored posts. It is important that you have managed to strike a balance between the posts that you write and the sponsored posts. If you start sharing too many sponsored posts, then your readers will lose interest and this isn't the best way forward. You should share sponsored posts in a strategic manner and don't make the content of the sponsored posts seem too bland or boring.

Promoting affiliate products

Promoting affiliate products will also help you in making money. Make sure that you are promoting only such products that you have used and such products that you know will help your audience. If you are looking for ways in which you can start promoting affiliate products or are searching for affiliate products, then you will need to start researching.

You will need to search for companies whose products you make use of and see if they offer any affiliate opportunities. Focusing on the products that your audience needs and wants will help you in becoming successful. Becoming an Amazon Associate will also help you in making money by promoting products that you use. You can start promoting such products on any of your social media profiles and share them with their affiliate link.

In addition, writing up honest reviews will help in attracting and retaining the trust of your consumers. Another way in which you can promote affiliate products is by creating a Resources page. This will help you in giving a detailed list of all the things that you make use of for running your blog and the different products that you promote.

Becoming a social media manager

Social media management has become a great job. Small and large businesses alike are making use of social media more than they ever did. This opens up jobs for those who are good at managing profiles across different social media sites. The best way to go about this would be to subscribe to a career website and then look out for any job postings or any other freelancing jobs.

Promoting your own services

You can make use of social media for promoting the services that you are offering. Social media will help in connecting you with your ideal audience. You can promote your services quite easily by including information about the same into your blog posts and so on.

Chapter Eleven:

What Separates Snapchat from Other Social Media

Snapchat was launched in the year 2011. However, its presence wasn't felt until the year 2013. Facebook had tried and miserably failed to snub it. Brands have been kind of slow in embracing this particular platform. Snapchat is a messaging app that allows the users to send snaps in the forms of photos or videos that will be automatically destructed after being viewed.

This platform is available for only smartphones. The sender has the option of selecting the amount of time for which the snap can be viewed and then the snap will be gone forever.

The one feature that helps in making Snapchat different from other social media networks is that it has an ability to form a personal connection with the receiver. Unlike the other social networking sites where the posts are public, when a snap is delivered it seems more tailor-made and personal.

A snap can be sent to a whole group, but even then, it has the personal touch to it. This gives the business an ability to form a personal bond with someone. Snaps received from someone else cannot be forwarded. This ensures that the content is fresh and unique. Snapchat stands apart from Facebook,

Chapter Eleven: What Separates Snapchat from Other Social Media

Twitter, or any other social media platform because it helps the businesses in interacting with their consumers in a personal and jovial manner.

The age groups between 13 and 25 cannot be easily reached on popular networking platforms like Facebook or Twitter. Snapchat helps in appealing to a much younger audience and this can be made use of by brands for approaching the audience they could never have reached before.

The features provided by Snapchat keep on increasing. Snapchat allows the user to create a good narrative in the form of stories. These stories could be pictures or video clips that have been strung together. This can be viewed multiple times within the time frame of 24 hours. After this time period is over, the clip would be automatically removed. Being able to build a narrative does go a long way when you are trying to engage your audience.

This helps in keeping your audience engaged all day long. If you are inclined towards making use of Snapchat for your marketing campaign then you will need to keep its time limit feature in view. The reason Snapchat has gained popularity is because of the time span that helps in grabbing viewer's attention. All the security breaches of data have made Internet users quite skeptical about the information that is shared on major social networking platforms.

When it comes to Snapchat, it helps in building their confidence since the data that they are sharing will not be available after the expiration of the time limit. You will not have to sort through millions of messages on a platform like Snapchat.

Engaging a small audience is really important for businesses. It is as important as garnering the attention of a larger audience. It is not just about the number of followers that you have got, it is also about the number of followers who care. The number of followers you have managed to engage with your content matters. The one to one experience that Snapchat helps in creating is a great way for achieving higher rates of engagement. This perceived intimacy is quite helpful.

Chapter Twelve:

Identifying a Target Audience

Before you can get started with creating some exciting content, you will need to direct your attention towards finding and building your audience. For building an audience, you will need to decide your target. Snapchat doesn't cater to all audiences, it is a good marketing tool, but it might not work for all forms of business.

As mentioned earlier, Snapchat appeals to the younger demographic. If your target audience is within the 13-26 age bracket, then you can make use of it.

If you are new to Snapchat, then the earlier chapters have all the basic information that you would require for getting started with it. It is good to know how you can find people or different businesses on Snapchat. However, you should also be concerned about making sure that people are able to find your brand or business and are adding you as well.

Building an audience for yourself shouldn't be too difficult if you have managed to create an active and engaged audience for yourself on various other social networking platforms. If individuals who are following you on other social media sites are also present on Snapchat, it is likely that they would have added you.

The groundwork is already done and you will simply need to inform your followers that you are on Snapchat and ask them to follow you. You can post information about the same on various other social media accounts of yours for alerting your followers.

The easiest way in which you can find your audience on Snapchat would be by posting your Snapchat username on your other accounts on social media and motivate your audience to add you. Include this information in your bios on other social networking platforms and new people can keep on adding you. When you post on different social media accounts for announcing your presence on Snapchat, your outreach will keep on increasing.

It is not just about posting information about your Snapchat account; you should also encourage people to add you. You will need to engage your audience. Keep posting interesting things and come up with new ways to make your audience feel involved in what you are doing.

There are different ways in which you can engage your audience on Snapchat and you have learned these methods in the previous chapters.

Chapter Thirteen:

Snapchat Lenses, Filters and Settings

Snapchat is an app meant to help people have fun with their pictures and videos. One of the prominent features of Snapchat is the lens that can be used for enhancing the quality of a picture. Let us take a look at this feature in detail

Snapchat lenses are quite easy to add to pictures, all you need to do is press and hold the picture and the app will automatically determine where to place the filter. This makes your job easier as you do not have to place the filters manually. Remember that these filters can be placed on both snaps and videos. Some common lenses used are a butterfly crown, floral wreath, face swap, dog-ears and the rainbow one.

Filters help you write on top of a picture or video. It also provides a place to add a caption or tagline. This is useful, as it will tell the other person what you are trying to do in the picture. Just like with a lens you can swipe right or left to find the filter of choice and place it on top of the picture or video. Once there, fill in whatever you want to add as the caption.

Check filters

It can sometimes get confusing when you have to pick between two great filters. For this, test both and settle for the one you think suits the picture best. For example, press the screen and use to place two filters before choosing the one that stays. This is great for all those that cannot choose between two or more filters. You can also place stickers on your pictures. Just click on the emoji option next to the T and add it to the picture on top.

Emojis

The emojis on Snapchat are versatile and there are many options to choose from too. Apart from adding them to your pictures and videos, they can also be added to objects in your pictures. This means that you need not pin the emojis to people alone and can also go on objects that are there in your photo.

This makes the photos and videos a little more personal and interesting for the viewers. They can be pinned wherever you would like them to be in the picture or video.

Songs

Songs and music are a big part of Snapchat videos. They enhance the quality and feel of the videos. Although Snapchat does not have an added audio feature, it is pretty simple to incorporate music into your videos. Record the video with the music playing in the background and Snapchat will record and add it to the background.

Music

It is also possible for you to turn off the music. In order to switch it off, record the video with the sound, as that will be an option. Now you will find the volume option at the bottom shaped like a loudspeaker. Press once to switch it off and an X will appear in front of it to signify that the volume has been turned off. The video will now not play the sound when it is viewed.

Chapter Fourteen:

Snapchat Tips and Tricks

Snapchat discover

Snapchat discover is a unique feature on Snapchat designed to help you keep tabs on magazines, websites and other such channels that you wish to follow. Snapchat helps in providing all the different channels and apps in one place so that you don't have to download the individual apps.

Right from Cosmopolitan to Buzzfeed to MTV, there is a lot to choose from and clicking on them will give you all the latest news and gossip. You will also be able to access live stories and other such fun content without having to leave the app. You don't have to always click on the individual apps and can press it down to subscribe to the individual channels. The latest news from the site will automatically update without you having to manually look for it.

This feature makes it extremely convenient for people to keep track of all the latest events and happenings around them. All the features are professionally curated to make it look great. You will have the chance to use it as inspiration and come up with great content yourself to share with friends and followers.

Updating

You have the choice to manually update Snapchat if you like. Although it generally updates automatically, you can manually look for any updates on the play store. Click the update button to do the needful and your Snapchat will be updated. If you are unable to do so then move to your settings and check if you have chosen to receive automatic updates. If not, then enable the option to automatically update your Snapchat.

Secret screenshot

You can secretly screenshot people's pictures without them knowing anything about it. Here are the steps to follow for the same. Start by loading the snap but don't open it. If it has automatically loaded then do not open it. Once you load the image, go to notifications, and switch on the airplane mode. Once airplane mode is on tap the Snapchat button and opens it. Screenshot using the usual method.

Now exit the app and ensure it is not running in the background. IOS users can double-click on the home button and swipe the app to close it. Android users can do this in the multitasking window and close it. Now deactivate airplane mode and close Snapchat. You can now open Snapchat and carry on as usual.

Assign numbers

It is obvious that we will have a few best friends in our lists. This refers to those that we regularly message. You have the option of changing their numbers in order to message them easily. Snapchat automatically assigns numbers to the ones that you message regularly.

It generally assigns the number 3 but this can be changed to a 5 or 7 depending on what you would like to assign to it. This will make it easier for you to message these people without looking for them in your friend list.

Deleting your account

If for some reason you do not wish to maintain your account owing to security reasons then you have the choice to delete it. Log in to your account and choose the delete option. This will delete your account for good. You will be able to create another account using a different username.

However, remember, once you delete your account, it cannot be undone, and you cannot retrieve the same. You will have to create a new one with a new username.

Travel mode

You have the option of picking travel mode on your Snapchat account in order to prevent automatic download of pictures and videos. This is great for all those whose phone batteries tend to drain away fast. Performing this simple trick can help you save on battery life and not have to worry about unwanted pictures downloading on your phone.

Choose the ones you wish to download and get stored on your phone. To enable the travel mode, go to settings and then to "manage." There you will find the option of "additional services" where you will find travel mode. Click on it to enable it.

Deleting snaps

It is possible for you to delete a single snap from a story. This is useful for all those that tend to add in several pictures and then trim it down to size. For this, choose the picture you would like to delete and swipe it upwards. The delete button will appear on top and pressing it will remove that particular picture from the story. A pop-up will ask if you surely want to delete the picture and choosing delete again will make the snap disappear.

Content from outside Snapchat

Now you may wonder if you are only allowed to upload those snaps and videos on Snapchat that were created using Snapchat tools. The answer is no, you don't have to rely on Snapchat alone for creating your snaps and videos. It is also possible for you to upload content that was created using external apps.

There are many third party apps that will help you create snaps and videos using your camera and then save it to your camera roll. The same can be uploaded to your Snapchat account.

Reusing snaps

It is possible for you to make use of old snaps and videos and repost them with new content such as lenses and filters. This will be helpful for those that want to keep it interesting and unique but don't have the time to take new pictures. All you have to do is tap on the download arrow once the snap has been taken.

This will save the picture for you. If you wish to download an entire story, then head over to the dots on the right of the story screen and choose the download button to download the story. Once done, add any filters and lens you like or modify it in any other way you like before uploading it.

Here are some general tips on how you can make your snaps look clear and nice.

Camera

First and foremost, get yourself a smartphone with a good quality camera. It is important to have a front facing camera, as you will be able to see the snap being taken. Although a good back camera with flash will also work, you will have to take multiple snaps to pick the best one.

If you will be using Snapchat to promote your products and services then it will be best to do some research on the best phone or tablet to pick. You also have the option of using a good quality external camera to take the pictures and then upload to your Snapchat account.

Lighting

The next aspect to bear in mind is the lighting. The lighting can play a big part in making or breaking the perfect picture. You have to take the picture in a bright spot. However, make sure it is not too bright, as it will create a bright light on your face. Trial and error is a must in order to find the right angle and lighting for your face.

Nothing beats sunlight or natural light as it provides just the right amount of brightness. If you are trying to photograph an object then place it in an appropriate place before taking the picture.

Editors

Make use of editors to enhance the picture quality. There are different external applications that can be made use of for editing photos. However, with Snapchat, different editors have been provided within the app itself. These will add a little bit of finesse to your pictures.

Filters and lens

The last step is to make use of filters and lenses. These will help a picture look interesting and fun. There are different filters to choose from and they are all fun to use. Choose whatever you think will look best.

These form the different criteria to bear in mind while taking the perfect snap.

Monetize Your Snapchat Account

These above-mentioned tips come in handy when you want to monetize your account. For doing this, you have to upload good quality pictures that are able to captivate the imagination of people and potential advertisers.

Here is how you can monetize your Snapchat account.

Step 1: The first step is to create content that will grab the viewer's attention. This can range from trying on makeup products to sporting clothes and accessories to reviewing products.

Step 2: The next step would be to get noticed by companies that will sponsor your pictures and videos.

Step 3: Once they approach you, look at the terms and conditions they have and go through all of it in detail. Once you are satisfied with it, you can sign up with them.

Step 4: They will provide the basis for videos and snaps they expect from you. You will have to adhere to their requirements and upload the same.

Step 5: You will be paid for your work based on the agreement you have with them.

This is a really good way to monetize if you have a large number of followers following your Snapchat account.

Conclusion

I would like to thank you once again for purchasing this book and I hope that you received valuable information out of it!

The main aim of this book was to help you learn the basics of Snapchat and teach you the different ways in which you can use it to your own advantage. You definitely will have learned new things through this book and must be eager to put them into practice. Every business would want to increase their customer base and improve their sales. Snapchat can be made use of for achieving these two goals for your business and do so much more.

Finally, if you enjoyed this book, then I'd like to ask you for a favor, would you be kind enough to leave a review for this book on Amazon? It'd be greatly appreciated!

I hope you fulfill all your business goals by making use of this app. Good luck!

www.ingramcontent.com/pod-product-compliance
Lightning Source LLC
Chambersburg PA
CBHW071807170526
45167CB00003B/1210